ER 551.567 ASP
Aspen-Baxter, Linda.
Rainbow

RAINBOWS

FOUNTAINDALE PUBLIC LIBRARY DISTRICT
300 West Briarcliff Road
Bolingbrook, IL 60440-2894
(630) 759-2102

Linda Aspen-Baxter
and Heather Kissock

MEDIA ENHANCED BOOKS
AV2 BY WEIGL™
ADDED VALUE • AUDIO VISUAL

www.av2books.com

MEDIA ENHANCED BOOKS
AV2 BY WEIGL™
ADDED VALUE • AUDIO VISUAL

Go to **www.av2books.com**, and enter this book's unique code.

BOOK CODE

M 9 2 8 7 6 1

AV2 by Weigl brings you media enhanced books that support active learning.

AV2 provides enriched content that supplements and complements this book. Weigl's AV2 books strive to create inspired learning and engage young minds in a total learning experience.

Your AV2 Media Enhanced books come alive with...

Audio
Listen to sections of the book read aloud.

Video
Watch informative video clips.

Embedded Weblinks
Gain additional information for research.

Try This!
Complete activities and hands-on experiments.

Key Words
Study vocabulary, and complete a matching word activity.

Quizzes
Test your knowledge.

Slide Show
View images and captions, and prepare a presentation.

...and much, much more!

Published by AV2 by Weigl
350 5th Avenue, 59th Floor New York, NY 10118
Website: www.av2books.com   www.weigl.com

Copyright ©2012 AV2 by Weigl
All rights reserved. No part of this publication may be reproduced, stored in a retrieval system, or transmitted in any form or by any means, electronic, mechanical, photocopying, recording, or otherwise, without the prior written permission of the publisher.

Library of Congress Cataloging-in-Publication Data

Kissock, Heather.
Rainbow / Heather Kissock and Linda Aspen-Baxter.
   p. cm. -- (Looking at the sky)
ISBN 978-1-61690-957-4 (hardcover : alk. paper) -- ISBN 978-1-61690-603-0 (online)
1. Rainbows--Juvenile literature. I. Linda Aspen-Baxter II. Title.
QC976.R2K575 2012
551.56'7--dc23
                        2011023438

Printed in the United States of America in North Mankato, Minnesota
1 2 3 4 5 6 7 8 9 0 15 14 13 12 11

062011
WEP030611

Senior Editor: Heather Kissock Art Director: Terry Paulhus

Weigl acknowledges Getty Images as the primary image supplier for this title.

RAINBOWS

CONTENTS

FOUNTAINDALE PUBLIC LIBRARY DISTRICT
300 West Briarcliff Road
Bolingbrook, IL 60440-2894
(630) 759-2102

4

We can see rainbows
in the sky when it rains.

A rainbow can be seen
when the Sun shines
on raindrops in the sky.

The Sun's light is made up of many colors. These colors appear in a rainbow.

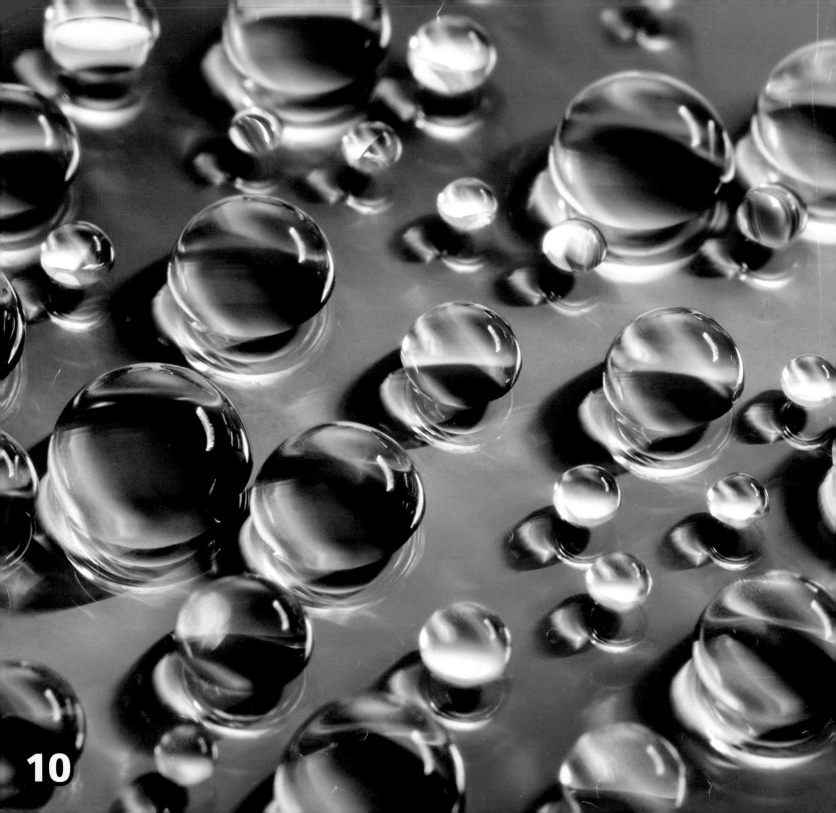

10

When the Sun's light enters
a raindrop, it makes seven colors.

The seven colors of a rainbow are red, orange, yellow, green, blue, indigo, and violet.

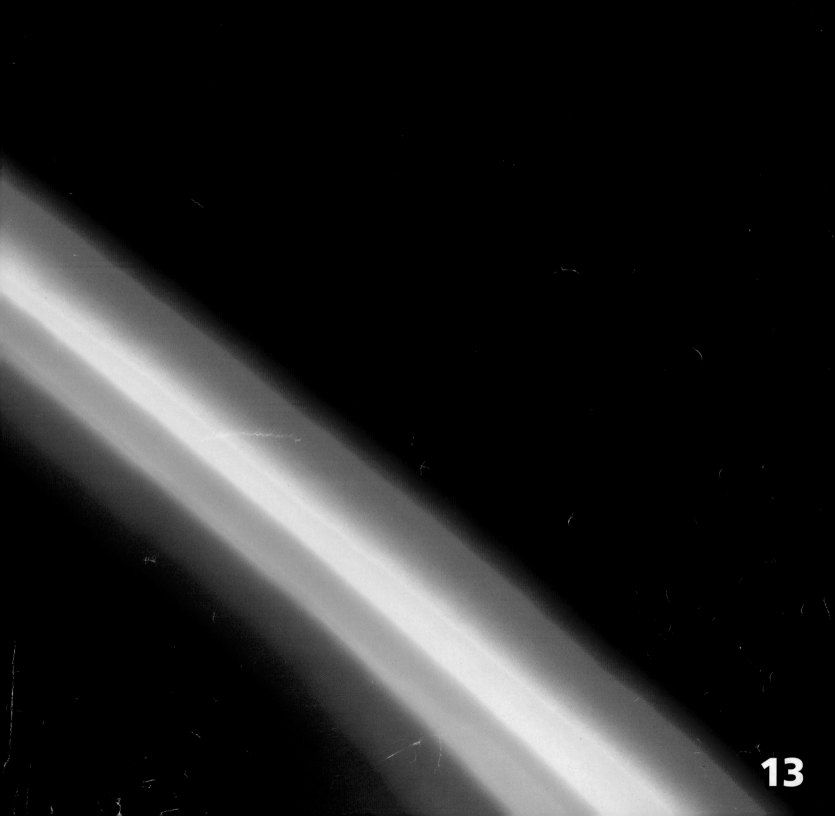
13

When you see a rainbow,
the Sun is behind you.

There can be two rainbows
in the sky at the same time.

17

Sometimes, rainbows appear when it has not rained. They can be seen in fountains and in the spray from a garden hose.

20

Rainbow colors can also appear in soap bubbles.

RAINBOW FACTS

This page provides more detail about the interesting facts found in the book. Simply look at the corresponding page number to match the fact.

Pages 4-5

We can see rainbows in the sky when it rains. Nature creates rainbows in the sky. They can be found almost anywhere in the world where there is rain. They appear after a rainstorm, when the Sun is shining.

Pages 6–7

A rainbow can be seen when the Sun shines on raindrops in the sky. Rainbows form when rain falls in one part of the sky while the Sun shines in another. Billions of raindrops are needed to make a rainbow.

Pages 8–9

The Sun's light is made up of many colors. These colors appear in a rainbow. The Sun's light is often referred to as white light. This light is made up of many colors of light that people can see as well as other colors that cannot be seen. When all colors are mixed together, sunlight looks white. When sunlight shines through raindrops, however, the colors separate.

Pages 10–11

When the Sun's light enters a raindrop, it makes seven colors. Sunlight follows a straight line when it moves through the air. When it enters water, it slows down and bends, or refracts. This bending creates the seven colors of the rainbow.

Pages 12–13

The seven colors of a rainbow are red, orange, yellow, green, blue, indigo, and violet. When a single rainbow is seen, red is at the top, and violet is at the bottom. This is because violet light bends more than any other color, while red bends the least.

Pages 14–15

When you see a rainbow, the Sun is behind you. A rainbow always appears in the sky opposite the Sun. After sunlight is bent inside raindrops, it is reflected back toward the Sun. We see the colors as they reflect back from the raindrops.

Pages 16–17

There can be two rainbows in the sky at the same time. One arches over the other. When this occurs, the lower rainbow is called the primary rainbow. The higher one is the secondary rainbow. The colors of a secondary rainbow are reversed. Violet is at the top, and red is at the bottom.

Pages 18–19

Sometimes, rainbows appear when it has not rained. Rain is not necessary for rainbows to appear. Rainbows can be seen whenever there is moisture in the air. This includes fountains, waterfalls, and the spray from a garden hose. As the Sun shines on the water drops, rainbows form.

Pages 20–21

Rainbow colors can also appear in soap bubbles. These are not true rainbows, however. Unlike rainbows, colors in bubbles can shift and change. They swirl with the movement of the liquid they are in. When people look at this type of rainbow, the colors may change, depending on the point of view.

WORD LIST

Research has shown that as much as 65 percent of all written material published in English is made up of 300 words. These 300 words cannot be taught using pictures or learned by sounding them out. They must be recognized by sight. This book contains 32 common sight words to help young readers improve their reading fluency and comprehension. This book also teaches young readers several important content words. These words are paired with pictures to aid in learning and improve understanding.

Page	Sight Words First Appearance
5	can, in, it, see, the, we, when
6	a, be, on
9	is, light, made, many, of, these, up
11	makes
12	and, are
15	you
16	at, same, there, time, two
18	has, from, not, sometimes, they
21	also

Page	Content Words First Appearance
5	rainbows, sky
6	raindrops, Sun
9	colors
18	fountains, hose, spray
21	bubbles

Check out av2books.com for activities, videos, audio clips, and more!

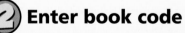

1 Go to av2books.com

2 Enter book code M 9 2 8 7 6 1

3 Fuel your imagination online!

www.av2books.com